Hello Lovely!

ALSO BY LANG LEAV

Self-Love for Small-Town Girls

The Gift of Everything

September Love

Poemsia: A Novel

Love Looks Pretty on You

Sea of Strangers

Sad Girls: A Novel

The Universe of Us

Memories

Lullabies

Love & Misadventure

Hello Lovely!

Inspirational quotes & poems on life, love & empowerment

LANG LEAV

Andrews McMeel
PUBLISHING®

Andrews McMeel Publishing
a division of Andrews McMeel Universal
1130 Walnut Street, Kansas City, Missouri 64106
www.andrewsmcmeel.com

25 26 27 28 29 TEN 10 9 8 7 6 5 4 3 2 1

ISBN: 979-8-8816-0012-9

Library of Congress Control Number: 2024945531

Editor: Patty Rice
Art Director/Designer: Diane Marsh
Production Editor: David Shaw
Production Manager: Shona Burns

ATTENTION: SCHOOLS AND BUSINESSES
Andrews McMeel books are available at quantity discounts with bulk purchase for educational, business, or sales promotional use. For information, please email the Andrews McMeel Publishing Special Sales Department: sales@andrewsmcmeel.com.

Dear Reader,

Do you remember a time when a quote changed your life? I do.

It happened in my late twenties when I had abandoned all hope of my dreams ever coming to fruition. One night, while feeling lost, I was scrolling aimlessly online, when a few simple lines stopped me in my tracks. It was the following quote by the late trailblazing tennis champion, Arthur Ashe: "Start where you are. Use what you have. Do what you can." At any other time, I might have scrolled right past it, but at that precise moment, those words struck me to my core.

It was exactly what I needed to see at that crucial point in my life.

The next morning, I followed the quote's advice: "Start where you are. Use what you have. Do what you can." With this mantra in mind, I posted my poems online.

Within days, a literary blog shared my work, and my poems went viral. I watched in wonder as my readership grew into the hundreds, then thousands, and eventually hundreds of thousands. This led to the publication of my first book, *Love & Misadventure*, which became an instant bestseller. Over the next decade, I exceeded my wildest dreams: having multiple books of poetry and novels published, traveling the world, and meeting my wonderful readers at festivals and signings—some of whom, like me, had their lives changed by a quote. Only in their case, it was one of mine.

I hope you find many lines in this book that resonate with you. More than that, I hope there will be a quote within these pages that finds you at the exact time it is meant to.

With all my love,

IF THEY WERE MEANT TO BE IN YOUR

LIFE, NOTHING COULD EVER MAKE THEM

LEAVE. IF THEY WEREN'T, NOTHING IN

THE WORLD COULD MAKE THEM STAY.

MEANT TO BE, SEA OF STRANGERS

SHE CAN FEEL IT DOWN TO HER VERY CORE—

this is her time.

SHE WILL NOT ONLY CLIMB MOUNTAINS—

she will move them too.

———————

HER TIME, THE UNIVERSE OF US

To me, a meaningful poem is the coming together of elements that are not necessarily exclusive to the words before you on paper. I am sure we have all experienced that wonderful rush when you stumble on a particular poem, and it suddenly becomes the center of gravity, drawing everything in your internal and external world, anchoring it in that moment.

I REALIZED WHAT I WANTED WAS TO BE YOU IN OUR RELATIONSHIP. I WANTED SOMEONE TO TAKE CARE OF ME THE WAY I HAVE TAKEN CARE OF YOU.

TO BE YOU, SELF-LOVE FOR SMALL-TOWN GIRLS

All this time,
I thought I was writing
for the LOVERS,
when I've been writing
for the WRITERS.

Don't stay where you are needed. Go where you are loved.

I think poetry is the most beautiful expression of language and in its purest form, is emotion transferred into words. It's almost like poets are running around with metaphorical nets and we're catching these feelings and transcribing them.

The only thing worse than saying goodbye is not getting the chance to say it.

POEMSIA: A NOVEL

A BOOK TRAVELS FOR DAYS, FOR YEARS, SOMETIMES FOR CENTURIES to MEET YOU AT AN EXACT POINT IN TIME.

INTRODUCTION, THE UNIVERSE OF US

WHERE THEY DESTROY,

we create;

WHERE THEY CRITICIZE,

we inspire.

THAT IS WHY THEY ARE THE CRITICS,

and we are the poets.

WE THE POETS, SEA OF STRANGERS

Comfort, security, companionship—almost anything can be mistaken for love. But only if you've never been in love.

———————————

ALMOST ANYTHING, SELF-LOVE FOR SMALL-TOWN GIRLS

Look at you. You've stitched your life so perfectly together. You worked so damn hard to get to where you are, and now have everything you ever wanted. So why do you keep looking back at the one thing that can undo it all?

———————————

THE ONE THING, SEA OF STRANGERS

We're kids, aren't we?
Yes, kids with
grown-up powers.

US, LULLABIES

The time and care you put into things will never go unnoticed. The universal ledger keeps count of every good deed you have done and will reward you accordingly. But only if it comes from a place of love and not obligation. With sweet gratitude and not resentment.

———————————

GOOD DEEDS, SELF-LOVE FOR SMALL-TOWN GIRLS

THE NOVELIST STRUGGLES.

The poet suffers.

Sometimes the loneliest place to be is in love.

THE LONELIEST PLACE, THE UNIVERSE OF US

You may have known them all your life or you may have barely known them at all. Either way, it is irrelevant—you cannot control the depth of a wound another inflicts upon you.

BROKEN HEARTS, LULLABIES

"

IN THE WRONG HANDS, YOUR PAST IS a WEAPON.

"

THE DISTANCE FROM YOU IS MEASURED

IN HOW FAR I'VE COME.

FROM YOU, SEA OF STRANGERS

"Pick yourself up. Get it together. Not because others have it worse than you. Not because you owe it to anyone to put on a smile. But because you have your mother's blood flowing through your veins. And even if you think otherwise, you matter to so many people. But first of all, you need to matter to yourself.

———————————

TO YOURSELF, SEPTEMBER LOVE

English is not my first language, but it is my first love.

Losing someone isn't an occasion or an event.

It doesn't just happen once. It happens over

and over again.

———————————

LOSING YOU, LULLABIES

AS A REFUGEE, IT IS COMMON TO FEEL

DISPLACED AND UNWANTED.

NOTHING AGES YOU LIKE SUFFERING.

There will come a time when your journey will matter less than imparting what you've learned to those who wish to follow in your footsteps.

IF A BOY EVER SAYS, YOU REMIND ME OF

SOMEONE—DON'T FALL IN LOVE WITH

HIM. YOU WILL NEVER BE ANYTHING

MORE THAN SECOND BEST.

FOREWARNED, LULLABIES

The most important advice I received was to write the book you want to write, rather than chasing trends or aiming solely for critical and commercial success. Such success is often unpredictable and largely dependent on luck. Instead, focus on writing authentically for yourself, rather than trying to cater to a specific audience. If your writing is genuine and true to your own voice, your audience will naturally find you.

It is your right
TO ENDLESSLY CURATE YOUR LIFE.

"

You're young and there's still so much ahead. So much uncertainty and doubt. It keeps you up at night—this wild, restless feeling. But you don't know how free you are. For this short, miraculous time, you have no one to answer to, nothing to lose. You belong wholly to yourself. And even though some days you wish your world would stop spinning for a second, to let you catch your breath— believe me, someday you're going to look back on this and you're going to miss this feeling.

"

YOUTH, LOVE LOOKS PRETTY ON YOU

After all, you are a woman,
and long before they punish you
for what you've done, they will
punish you for what you are.

A WOMAN, SEPTEMBER LOVE

"

As a child of immigrants, I naturally assumed the role of translator for my parents. I learned very early on to simplify the language and hone it down to the bare essentials.

"

My father once told me a story about an old redwood tree—how she stood tall and proud—her sprawling limbs clothed in emerald green. With a smile, he described her as a mere sapling, sheltered by her elders and basking in the safety of the warm, dappled light. But as this tree grew taller, she found herself at the mercy of the cruel wind and the vicious rain. Together, they tore at her pretty boughs until she felt as though her heart would split in two.

After a long, thoughtful pause, my father turned to me and said, "My daughter, one day the same thing will happen to you. And when that time comes, remember the redwood tree. Do not worry about the cruel wind or the vicious rain—but do as that tree did and just keep growing."

THE REDWOOD TREE, THE UNIVERSE OF US

My father was a house,

my mother was a home.

SHELTER, SEA OF STRANGERS

I've never met you before,

but I recognize this feeling.

———————————

RECOGNITION, THE UNIVERSE OF US

There is a girl who never returns her library books.

Don't give her your heart—it is unlikely you will ever

see it again.

———————————————

A CAUTIONARY TALE, LULLABIES

ALL LOVE IS FLEETING—
even when it
lasts a lifetime.

FLEETING, SEPTEMBER LOVE

SOMEONE ONCE TOLD ME WRITING IS

LIKE PANNING FOR GOLD. BUT I THINK

IT IS LIKE STUMBLING ON THE RUINS OF

A LOST CITY, TALKING TO ITS GHOSTS.

WANDERING ITS DESERTED STREETS

WITH LONG-FORGOTTEN NAMES.

THE PATH OF A WRITER, SEPTEMBER LOVE

I think sadness adds something to literature that is wholly unique. It's like an ingredient—like salt—it completely transforms a dish. I think that's the powerful effect that sadness has on literature.

I wanted everything

BECAUSE I DIDN'T WANT ANYTHING ENOUGH.

I learned that writing is the consolation prize you are given when you don't get the thing you want the most.

SAD GIRLS: A NOVEL

Nothing is beneath you. And if you believe this with your whole heart—believe every living soul should be treated with respect and kindness—you will realize it goes the other way. For once you truly believe no one is beneath you—you will see no one is above.

ABOVE YOU, SEPTEMBER LOVE

I believe if you have a real passion for writing, it's something you will naturally pursue, no matter the obstacles that are placed in your path. Throughout my life, I have gone through so many renditions of my creative self, only to arrive exactly where I had started.

ASK YOUR INNER CHILD, *WHAT DO YOU*

WANT ME TO DO FOR YOU TODAY?

Give them all time in the world to answer.

AND THEN DO WHAT THEY ASK.

INNER CHILD, SELF-LOVE FOR SMALL-TOWN GIRLS

Emotions are delicate and complex, vast and wide ranging, made up of layers upon layers of feeling, often conflicting. At times, it seems these sentiments exist purely to confuse and unsettle you. But occasionally, an emotion will seize you so completely, hold you so firmly in its grasp, that you cannot mistake it for any other thing. In these moments, you must follow its lead, go where it wants to take you. It is a directive from your heart that you cannot ignore.

COMPLEX EMOTIONS, SELF-LOVE FOR SMALL-TOWN GIRLS

You must believe it is your destiny to create beauty in this world. To shape your life with love and purpose, touch it ever so briefly with your weary hands and leave it a little more cherished than it was.

———————

LEGACY, SEPTEMBER LOVE

" Your most dangerous self is your present self. The self that talks you out of doing what's hard in the moment. This is the self that must always be held accountable, kept in check. With time, consistent mastery of the present self will yield the best and brightest version of you. "

SELF-DOMINATION, SELF-LOVE FOR SMALL-TOWN GIRLS

There is a point in every relationship when you realize it's over and seldom is it the day you break up. For some, that moment is long after you say goodbye. For others, the moment is long before.

WHEN IT'S OVER, SEA OF STRANGERS

To Be a Poet You Must Hold Nothing Back.

IN POETRY THERE IS NO ROOM FOR EGO,

NOWHERE TO HIDE. YOU MUST WRITE

UNDER THE PRETENSE THAT NO ONE

WILL EVER READ A SINGLE WORD.

A SINGLE WORD, SEPTEMBER LOVE

YOU COULDN'T SAY IT WAS LOVE,

could you?

YOU COULDN'T SAY IT WASN'T, EITHER.

IT WAS LOVE, LOVE LOOKS PRETTY ON YOU

Remember, your words are your power. Never forget your words.

YOUR WORDS, THE UNIVERSE OF US

That's the thing about happiness. It doesn't require justification. When I'm happy, I'm happy. I don't feel the need to write about it.

WHEN I'M HAPPY, SEA OF STRANGERS

Every time I see my name, I hear it in your voice.

"

If I could tell my younger self one thing, it would be this: There are many things in life you can postpone, but love isn't one of them.

———————

THE NATURE OF LOVE, SEA OF STRANGERS

I couldn't figure out why love was different with you until I realized it hadn't been love with anyone else.

WITH ANYONE ELSE, SEA OF STRANGERS

"

I HAVE BEEN QUIET LATELY, I KNOW. NOT BECAUSE I DON'T HAVE ANYTHING TO SAY, BUT BECAUSE I HAVE TOO MUCH.

"

It should be my right to mourn someone who has

yet to leave this world but no longer wants to be

part of mine.

_____

NO LONGER MINE, SEA OF STRANGERS

"

Leave him, let him go. Don't be the crazy ex-girlfriend or the shoulder to cry on. You're more than just an ego boost, a story he can tell someone he's trying to impress. Just walk away with your head held high and don't give him another second of your time. I know you love him so much that every step is killing you. But this is the moment you'll always look back on as the day you put yourself first. Go and make something beautiful of your life and I promise you, one day you'll forget he was ever there.

"

MOVING ON, SEA OF STRANGERS

AS POETS, WE ARE CONSTANTLY
COLLABORATING WITH OUR PAST SELVES—
IT IS ONLY THROUGH OUR MEMORIES THAT
WE ARE ABLE TO BECOME FULLY FORMED IN
THE PRESENT. WE NEVER TRULY KNOW WHEN
SOMETHING WILL END. BUT BEGINNINGS
ARE MUCH EASIER TO RECOGNIZE.

INTRODUCTION, THE GIFT OF EVERYTHING

Poetry is the recognition of the disparate.

The arrangement of words that should not

otherwise belong together, yet once put side

by side leads us to question how they could

have ever been apart.

POETRY IS, SELF-LOVE FOR SMALL-TOWN GIRLS

Poetry should not center merely on the artful depiction of emotions, but the ability to express them in a way that is resonate and impactful.

CLOUD LAKE LITERARY: IN CONVERSATION WITH LANG LEAV

It was like hearing every goodbye ever said to me, said all at once.

THREE QUESTIONS, LULLABIES

It was words that I fell for. In the end, it was words

that broke my heart.

LANGUAGE, MEMORIES

Let time work its magic for you, my love. For you

have known the measure of what you have lost.

In time, those who know can forget. Those who

don't, cannot.

***

THOSE WHO KNOW, SELF-LOVE FOR SMALL-TOWN GIRLS

I write not to be known but to know myself.

WHY I WRITE, SEPTEMBER LOVE

You are made of all the things you have loved.

You are made of all the things you have lost.

And both contribute in equal measure to

your beauty and your brilliance.

———————————

ALL THE THINGS, SEPTEMBER LOVE

Who you LOVE and who loves you back determines so much in your LIFE.

WHO YOU LOVE, SEA OF STRANGERS

THE MEASURE OF MAN IS NOT

IN HOW HE LOVES YOU,

BUT HOW HE LETS YOU GO.

———————————

POSTED ON THREADS, 2:44 PM, MONDAY, JULY 8, 2024

Love looks pretty on you, and you should wear it with pride.

INTRODUCTION, LOVE LOOKS PRETTY ON YOU

Men don't compare us with other women. They compare us to an ideal.

AN IMPOSSIBLE IDEAL, SEA OF STRANGERS

"People will do all they can to reduce you, make you lesser than you are. But you have more than enough light, more than enough goodness to spare. They can take as much as they want, but it would be akin to scooping cupfuls of the ocean from someone like you. So, let them do their best and know despite all their efforts, they remain so impossibly, so laughably small.

MORE THAN ENOUGH, THE GIFT OF EVERYTHING

I OFTEN THINK OF WHERE YOU ARE
AND IF YOU'RE HAPPY.
Are you in love? I hope she is gentle.
I KNOW YOU AND I ARE THE
SAME IN THAT WAY—
we bruise a little more easily than most.
YOU SEE,
OUR SOULS WERE
made in the same breath.

A POSTCARD, THE UNIVERSE OF US

The further you get in life, the faster everything moves. You only get so much time to take everything in, to decide what to grasp, what to hold on to. There are things that you will miss. Do not spend too long on them. Sometimes, we make too much of what has gone. When life reveals itself to you, when it begins to unfold at a manic pace, you may only have a fraction of a second to make up your mind. The most important thing is that you do.

_____

DECISIONS, SELF-LOVE FOR SMALL-TOWN GIRLS

I know the rain does not discriminate between day or night but now, at this very moment, I feel like I am the sun.

HAPPINESS, MEMORIES

There it is, that one thing in your past you wish you could undo. It sits in your mind like a big, red, tantalizing bow. A gentle tug is all it would take to set things right. If only you could get to it. But you can't.

REGRETS, LOVE LOOKS PRETTY ON YOU

We all have moments of darkness, moments when we are so unlike ourselves. And like vultures they wait for a

slip, a misstep, then they take that part of us and try to convince the world that is all we are.

VULTURES, LOVE LOOKS PRETTY ON YOU

It's possible to move on from someone even if your heart refuses to let go. And it's not something you need to consciously do. It will just happen gradually, over time. The ache will always be there, but the intensity will fade, and you'll find other beautiful things to fill your days with.

———

THOUGHTS ON LETTING GO, SEA OF STRANGERS

I am in a
tug-of-war with
my past self.
We're fighting
over who gets
to keep you.

"

The sad thing is the moment you start to miss someone, it means they're already gone.

GONE, THE UNIVERSE OF US

"

We all become someone else's

version of ourselves.

———————————

EVENTUALLY, SELF-LOVE FOR SMALL-TOWN GIRLS

You attract what you write.

MANIFESTATION, SELF-LOVE FOR SMALL-TOWN GIRLS

Your love warms me the way I am warmed by the residual heat of the sun, a faraway benevolent love wishing only good things for me, the desire to see me grow without having to play a part in it.

———————————

ONLY GOOD THINGS, SELF-LOVE FOR SMALL-TOWN GIRLS

My mother once said to me there are two kinds of men you'll meet. The first will give you the life you want and the second will give you the love you desire. If you're one of the lucky few, you will find both in the one person. But if you ever find yourself having to choose between the two, then always choose love.

———————

CHOOSE LOVE, INTRO TO "WHO DO YOU LOVE" BY ALL SAINTS

I found that even in fiction, it is dangerous to stray too far from the truth.

"I will celebrate this life of mine, with or without you. The moon does not need the sun to tell her she is already whole.

MY LIFE, SEA OF STRANGERS

WHEN LOVE FINDS YOU, IT DOESN'T COME

WITH CRASHING WAVES OR THUNDERBOLTS.

IT APPEARS AS A SONG ON THE RADIO

OR A PARTICULAR BLUE IN THE SKY. IT

DAWNS ON YOU SLOWLY, LIKE A WARM

WINTER SUNRISE—WHERE THE PROMISE

OF SUMMER SHINES OUT FROM WITHIN.

HOPE, MEMORIES

We inhabit the same world but do not share a common reality.

DIVISION, THE GIFT OF EVERYTHING

Missing someone can *sometimes be the best thing* for a writer.

SAD GIRLS: A NOVEL

All these years later, I have stopped looking for answers. I know better now, that love is never a guarantee. Not when you have the rest of the world to contend with.

THE SADDEST THING, MEMORIES

I Don't Think you Need to Be in Love to write. But you Had to Have Been once.

ONCE IN LOVE, SEA OF STRANGERS

In every relationship, there is an underlying question we must keep asking ourselves:

How can we at once be in love and free?

IN LOVE AND FREE, SEPTEMBER LOVE

YOUR FIRST LOVE ISN'T THE FIRST

PERSON YOU GIVE YOUR HEART TO—

IT'S THE FIRST ONE WHO BREAKS IT.

SAD GIRLS: A NOVEL

Last night I had a dream that felt like a memory. A glimpse of what could have been. Crossed signals from another life. Where instead of all this, I had you. And life was exquisitely simple. And we were desperately happy.

I HAD YOU, LOVE LOOKS PRETTY ON YOU

"As writers, we have a talent for inhabiting our bodies at different times. We can recall all those emotions, and they become the building blocks we use to express our feelings, even if they happened a long time ago or haven't happened yet."

IT IS IMPOSSIBLE TO KNOW WHETHER

YOU TRULY WANT SOMETHING UNTIL

THE MOMENT IT SLIPS INTO THE COLD,

HARD REALITY OF YOUR LIFE.

—————————

REMEMBER THIS, THE GIFT OF EVERYTHING

When we leave this world, we give up all our possessions and our memories. Love is the only thing we take with us. It is all we carry from one life to the next.

STARDUST, MEMORIES

Seriously, masculinity is overrated. Even Superman has a weakness.

POEMSIA: A NOVEL

The second I tried to tell myself I wasn't in love was

the moment I realized I was.

———————————

MOMENT OF TRUTH, THE UNIVERSE OF US

You only get one chance to fall in love with your heart still whole.

THE EDGE OF THE WORLD, THE UNIVERSE OF US

More love
is found in grief
than in love itself.

I AM THE

crazy cat lady

OF YOUR DREAMS.

POEMSIA: A NOVEL

"

You asked me to imagine what it must have been like, for the first two people who fell in love; before the word *love* was conceived. You said it felt like that for you. Like we existed in a time before love—as though we were waiting for the word to catch up to the feeling.

"

———

HOW WE BEGAN, THE *UNIVERSE* OF US

My life is beautiful because I say it is.

RESET, SELF LOVE FOR SMALL-TOWN GIRLS

That was the moment before everything. When I thought I was in love—when I had yet to feel the full force of it.

BEFORE LOVE, SEPTEMBER LOVE

There is one thing you should know about writing. It will inevitably lead you to dark places as you cannot write authentically about something unless you have lived it. However, you should always bear in mind that you are only a tourist and must always remain one. You were blessed with the gift of words, in order to bring a voice to suffering. But do not be too indulgent despite how addictive sadness can be, how easy it is to get lost down the path of self-destruction. You must emerge from adversity, scathed but victorious to tell your story and, in turn, light the way for others.

WRITING, SEA OF STRANGERS

I often wonder why we want so much, to give others the very thing that we were denied. The mother working tirelessly to provide her child with an education; the little boy who was bullied in school and is now a Nobel Prize–winning advocate for peace. The author who writes happy endings for the characters in her book.

THE VERY THING, LULLABIES

He stayed long enough *to make me think* he would never leave.

HE STAYED, THE GIFT OF EVERYTHING

Is it truly possible

to live without shame?

If not inflicted by others,

then self-imposed?

SHAME, SEPTEMBER LOVE

The less you speak,
the more weight
your words will
carry when you do.

I know you have seen things you wish you hadn't. You have done things you wish you could take back. And you wonder why you were thrown into the thick of it all—why you had to suffer the way you did. And as you are sitting there alone and hurting, I wish I could put a pen in your hand and gently remind you how the world has given you poetry and now you must give it back.

POETRY, MEMORIES

I don't know how you are so familiar to me—or why it feels less like I am getting to know you and more as though I am remembering who you are. How every smile, every whisper brings me closer to the impossible conclusion that I have known you before, I have loved you before—in another time, a different place—some other existence.

SOUL MATES, LOVE & MISADVENTURE

A girl from nowhere special. With a fistful of dirt in her hand. And an irrepressible fire in her belly.

Who looks up at the stars and knows them by heart. Who is patiently learning the language of The Universe.

And believes in something greater than herself. That loves her unconditionally.

And will carry her always. A girl who looks up at the stars knowing one day, she will be among them.

AMONG THE STARS, SEPTEMBER LOVE

"The truth is, those who lack authenticity, and write for all the wrong reasons, are building their future on shaky ground. If you have to steal from others to win, then you have already lost. Anything you gain, any sense of victory you feel, will be hollow because you know you haven't really earned it. You can convince the whole world, but the one person you'll never convince is yourself.

POEMSIA: A NOVEL

My absolute love and adoration for a man

can live in peace with my feminism.

FOR A MAN, SEPTEMBER LOVE

For many women, turning thirty is something we are conditioned to dread. As though we are born with a clock already ticking, counting down. From our first breath, we are in a race against time. I clearly remember my race. Looking at how far everyone had gone ahead of me, feeling panic well up in my chest. All my life, I had thought the clock ticking away inside me was a time bomb. But when the time came, I realized the clock wasn't counting down—it was counting up. And just like that, my whole life came together, and I knew it was just the beginning.

Everything good that happened after that would have happened anyway. But after thirty, I learned that when you confront your fear, it will no longer have power over you. And when you are no longer afraid, the possibilities are endless.

AFTER THIRTY, SEPTEMBER LOVE

How do I thank my mother for giving me the life she desperately wanted for herself?

Think of a moment in your life.

A singular fragment of your life.

How do you feel about it now?

How did you feel about it then?

———————————

GROWTH, SELF-LOVE FOR SMALL-TOWN GIRLS

I used to think love had no limits—but I draw the line at myself.

SELF-PRESERVATION, SEPTEMBER LOVE

Something I wish I had known from the beginning. If you are criticized for your writing, it means you are creating work of note. When you find yourself in a place where strangers are talking about you, keep creating the work that got you noticed. Do not alter your writing to appease your critics. It is natural to crave validation, especially from those who will never give it. To be a successful writer, you must ignore this instinct. This is the most critical lesson I have learned. You can't please everyone, so don't even try. This rule applies in life, in love, and especially in writing.

THE GOLDEN RULE, SEPTEMBER LOVE

YOUR NAME IS THE SECOND ONE

YOUR MOTHER GAVE YOU.

Love was the first.

MOTHERHOOD, SEPTEMBER LOVE

The world of dating and relationships can be daunting. Especially since your partner will play such a huge role in shaping your life. I think it's important to follow your heart, but also to listen to your head. You can't control who you fall in love with, but you can certainly choose who you want to have in your life. I hope my writing helps illustrate the beautiful, complex, and messy nature of love, with the underlying message that although love is powerful and intoxicating, you are more so. You can be in love and still be yourself. I think that's the most important thing for a woman to distinguish.

You said my sadness was like the sun, beautiful from a distance but it hurt you too much to come closer.

NOW AND THEN, MEMORIES

I wish I knew why he left. What his reasons were.

Why he changed his mind. For all these years, I have

turned it over in my head—all the possibilities—yet

none of them make any sense. And then I think,

perhaps it was because he never loved me. But that

makes the least sense of all.

REASONS, LULLABIES

LIFE WENT ON WITHOUT YOU.

OF COURSE, IT DID.
OF COURSE, IT DOES.

IT WAS JUST AN ENDING,
NOT THE END.

COLLISION, MEMORIES

"

It happens like this. One day you meet someone and for some inexplicable reason, you feel more connected to this stranger than anyone else—closer to them than your closest family. Perhaps because this person carries an angel within them—one sent to you for some higher purpose, to teach you an important lesson or to keep you safe during a perilous time.

What you must do is trust in them—even if they come hand in hand with pain or suffering—the reason for their presence will become clear in due time.

Though here is a word of warning—you may grow to love this person but remember they are not yours to keep. Their purpose isn't to save you but to show you how to save yourself. And once this is fulfilled, the halo lifts and the angel leaves their body as the person exits your life. They will be a stranger to you once more.

ANGELS, LOVE & MISADVENTURE

If this is my heartache, then let it be mine to endure. Permit me to feel it in its entirety. Don't tell me how much of you I am allowed to love.

———————————

MY HEARTACHE, THE UNIVERSE OF US

I HAVE BURIED MYSELF SO DEEP IN MY WORDS THAT SOMETIMES I CAN'T TELL IF I AM THE PERSON WRITING OR THE ONE HIDING BETWEEN THE LINES.

Thank you for allowing me time to make myself whole, to learn how to love myself again the way you have loved me all these years with such tender conviction, for never asking anything of me, for never once withholding. Thank you for loving me and for letting me go.

———————————

LOVING ME, SELF-LOVE FOR SMALL-TOWN GIRLS

Why is it every time we say good night, it feels like goodbye?

SOULS, LOVE & MISADVENTURE

I believe we think more deeply about the universe

when we're falling in love. I think the mysterious pull

that draws you to another person is identical to the

one that moves our eyes upward to the stars.

———————————

INTRODUCTION, THE UNIVERSE OF US

Greet the world with no expectation.

Love as though you have never been hurt or betrayed.

Let go of the ones who take so much from
you yet offer nothing in return.

This is how you take back your power.

———————————

TAKE BACK YOUR POWER, SEA OF STRANGERS

Sometimes I am caught between poetry and prose,

like two lovers I can't decide between. Prose says

to me, let's build something long and lasting. Poetry

takes me by the hand, and whispers, *come with me,*

let's get lost for a while.

POETRY AND PROSE, SEA OF STRANGERS

Women are fierce. They are powerful. No matter what language they speak, how they dress, or the work they choose to do. What matters is they have a choice, and the freedom to carve out a life for themselves.

As long as we know women who are strong and resilient, we must respect them, carry them forward, lift them up.

For they are the product of all our other selves, the women we were, the ones we strive to be, the collective struggle of our mothers, our sisters, our daughters.

Our salvation will only come if we stand together.

———————————

WOMAN'S ANTHEM, LOVE LOOKS PRETTY ON YOU

There is so much beauty in not getting what you want. So much creation and art. You'd think that the universe withholds from you, just so it can witness what you will do with your longing; how you will fill in the missing parts.

MISSING PARTS, THE GIFT OF EVERYTHING

Everything I write is observational—even when it is my own self I am watching.

MY OWN SELF, THE GIFT OF EVERYTHING

Time is the best editor. To have an incubation period for your work is the ultimate luxury, and one I certainly did not possess while writing under the glare of the social media spotlight.

I don't think all writers are sad, I think it's the other way around—

all sad people write.

SAD GIRLS: A NOVEL

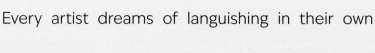

Every artist dreams of languishing in their own perceived genius, separate from the world and all the prying eyes. Every artist wants to hoard their creations without the need to sell off pieces of their soul. Deep down, every artist wishes they could remain undiscovered, like buried treasure.

EVERY ARTIST, SELF-LOVE FOR SMALL-TOWN GIRLS

Universal law dictates that not a soul can hurt you without first handing you the keys to their own destruction.

TODAY I WROTE IN MY JOURNAL

AFTER A LENGTHY HIATUS. THE FIRST

THING I THOUGHT TO WRITE WAS AN

EXPLANATION FOR MY ABSENCE.

Isn't That Strange?

THE NEED WE FEEL TO JUSTIFY OURSELVES

IS SO POWERFUL THAT WE DO IT EVEN

WHEN NO ONE IS WATCHING.

SELF-EXPLANATORY, SELF-LOVE FOR SMALL-TOWN GIRLS

In a dream I was at the banquet of your life, toasting you along with everyone else. I looked on, weak with pride, glowing with love as you, always gracious, always diligent, proceeded to thank everyone but me.

———————————

ACKNOWLEDGMENT, SELF-LOVE FOR SMALL-TOWN GIRLS

The simple truth remains that I have only written about what has happened or what almost did. I may dress it in a thousand different outfits, but every word is true and everyone is me.

FICTION, SELF-LOVE FOR SMALL-TOWN GIRLS

"You want to write for the world but you can't figure out what the world wants. If you write for a trend, it'll be over before you can get a word out. If you write for fame and fortune, your work will lack authenticity. So, remember, writing is a journey inward, not out. Write for the simple joy of knowing your own thoughts. Write for yourself. That is what the world wants."

WRITE FOR YOURSELF, LOVE LOOKS PRETTY ON YOU

Be patient. Your voice will find its way into the world, not in one loud instance but a steady trickle that turns into a deluge.

It is only the year that is ending. So why does it feel

like the world is?

DECEMBER, SEPTEMBER LOVE

Hello Lovely!

Acknowledgments

My heartfelt thanks to everyone who made this collection possible. To my agent, Alec, for your unwavering guidance and support; to my wonderful editor, Patty, with whom I've now completed a dozen cherished books (and counting!). To Kirsty, Kathy, and the entire team at Andrews McMeel, thank you for bringing my books to the world. A special thanks to Diane and the design team for bringing my words to life with such care and creativity. I am deeply grateful to my other half, Michael, for being my endless source of inspiration and always believing in me and my words.

About the Author

Novelist and poet Lang Leav was born in a refugee camp as her family fled the Khmer Rouge Regime. She spent her formative years in Sydney, Australia, in the predominantly migrant town of Cabramatta. Among her many achievements, Lang is the winner of a Qantas Spirit of Youth Award, Churchill Fellowship, and Goodreads Reader's Choice Award.

Lang has been featured on CNN, NPR, SBS Australia, Intelligence Squared UK, and Radio New Zealand, and in various publications, including Literary Hub, *Vogue*, *Newsweek*, the *Straits Times*, the *Guardian*, and the *New York Times*.